3

BIBLE STUDY

For Black Women

Workbook Edition

Daily Scripture Readings to Connect with God, Grow in Faith, and Let Go of Anxiety

Simone Bello

OAKRIDGE
PRESS

First Print Edition 2022

10 9 8 7 6 5 4 3 2 1

ISBN: 978-1-77434-132-2 (Paperback)

ISBN: 978-1-77434-133-9 (Ebook)

CONTENTS

Get Your Free Bonus!

As a thank you for picking up your copy of this book, we have included a free mini-book download for you.

The Law of Attraction: Manifest All of Your Wishes and Desires

Simply scan the QR code below using the camera of your smartphone:

How to Use This Book

This book is a short version bible study of the status quo year-long bible study. Its intention is to begin to build habits for women to study the bible religiously at least once a day.

In this one-month version, you will find
sections with different themes that relate to all our lives.
Set aside the next 30 days to use this book
once daily, either early to rise to before going to sleep at night.

What You'll Need:
_____

You may use any translation you choose, this
Bible study was based on the NIV.

No more than 10 minutes for each day.

A pen or pencil for the journal entries.

Day 1: Gratitude

Bible Reading: Psalm 34:1-4

One of the easiest ways to receive blessings from God is through gratitude. In our Bible reading for today, the psalmist decided always to bless the Lord at all times (Psalm 34:1). Perhaps you're going through some challenges right now; continue to say, "Thank you, Lord."

Our God can do all things (Jer. 32:27), and He can change all situations. He is greater than the greatest and mightier than the mightiest. When you continue to thank Him, things will begin to turn around for the better.

Unfortunately, the devil knows the benefits of showing gratitude to our Maker. That's why he'll keep shifting your focus to the things that are not working out yet in your life. As a result, you may begin to lose interest in Bible reading, fasting and prayer, and fellowship with the brethren,
If you find yourself in this situation, ask God for the grace to trust Him at all times.

Today, take some time to think about the goodness of God in your life and thank Him sincerely. Remember that if He did it before, He will do it again!

Prayer Point: Father, thank you for the wonderful things you have done in my life. Give me the grace to be grateful in both good and bad times, in Jesus' Name.

African American women are loved by God and are children of God. Make a list of some things you are grateful for in your life.

What goes gratitude towards God look like? Do you make a habit of expressing it?

Day 2: Forgive And Move On

Bible Reading: Matthew 6:15

Do you want God to forgive your sins, If yes, you need to forgive those who have offended you (Matt. 6:15). At some point in your Christian journey, your obedience to God will be tested through forgiveness. Only a few things in life hurt more than betrayal from a close friend or family member (Psalm 41:9). While it may seem as though the pain will last forever, trust me, it won't. When you refuse to let go of the past, it will be a hindrance to your prayer.

When you forgive, you also need to forget so that you won't keep replaying the scenario in your heart. So, if you've been praying about a particular situation without receiving answers, forgive everyone who has caused you pain.

Leave a message for the person who hurt you so much, telling them you have genuinely forgiven them. Allow God to fight for you, because vengeance belongs to him. From now on, you can go to God in prayer without feeling the guilt of not forgiving people for their sins. He will surely grant your desires speedily.

Prayer Point: Father, give me the grace to forgive everyone who has offended me. In the name of Jesus, answer every prayer that has been held up because I haven't forgiven.

What does forgiveness to the Lord look like? What does it not include?

- ---
--- ---

Is there someone in your life that you need to ask forgiveness? How is it affecting your relationship with Jesus?

- ---
--- ---

Day 3: Fear Not; God Is With You

Bible Reading: Isaiah 41:10

Fear is one of the instruments the devil uses in tormenting those who do not believe in God. There is nothing to be worried about if God is on your side. In Matthew 14:28-33, Jesus instructs Peter to approach him by walking on the water. When Peter focused his attention on Jesus, he was able to walk on the sea without any problem. However, as soon as Peter paid attention to the wind, he was afraid and began to drown.

Many Christians, similar to Peter, are preoccupied with their careers, marriages, finances, and the future rather than casting their cares upon God. In the long run, they become overwhelmed with life situations and may even develop health problems.

We have a Father who cares so much about his children. He has promised never to leave us nor forsake us. So, why should you be afraid of what tomorrow holds?

When God says, "Do not be afraid," it means you should keep your mind at ease, no matter the situation. Today, meditate on the promises of God, and fear will have no place in your heart.

Prayer Point: Heavenly Father, deliver me from the spirit of fear. Today, I am no longer a slave to fear because Jesus lives in my heart.

Do you experience the fear of physical appearance? Why or why not?

Describe something you do not like to admit you are afraid of
.

Day 4: The Holy Spirit, Our

Source of Inspiration

Bible Reading: Psalm 32:8

There is nothing we can do without the help of God. No matter how intelligent, good looking, educated, and financially stable you are, you will need help at some point in life.

In our bible reading for today (Psalm 32:8), God promised to instruct and teach you in the way you should go. But that's not all! He also promised to counsel you with his loving eyes on you.

Unfortunately, some believers do not open their hearts to the leading of the Holy Spirit. How do you get inspiration from God when you don't read the Bible, pray, or fast? Some believers constantly live a life of sin and expect the Holy Spirit to minister to them.

Paul the Apostle made it clear in Romans 6:1 that you can't live in sin and ask for more grace at the same time.

So if you lack inspiration in any area of your life, release yourself completely to the leading of the Holy Spirit. He will come through for you in unimaginable ways.

Prayer Point: Father, I have decided to follow your lead. Instruct and teach me in the way I should go in Jesus' Name.

What areas of your life has God inspired you to take care of?

Which African American public figure can we all draw inspiration from? What is it about this woman that is so inspiring?

Day 5: Love Your Neighbor

Bible Reading: John 15:12

In most of Jesus Christ's teachings, He emphasized the need to love one another. In the book of Luke 10:30-37, Jesus tells the story of a man who was attacked by robbers on his way to Jericho. The robbers not only stripped the man naked but also beat him and abandoned him for dead.
Surprisingly, a priest and a Levite saw this man and passed the other way. But when a Samaritan saw this man, who was attacked by robbers, he took care of his wounds, housed him, and paid the innkeeper to look after him.

We live in a world where people hardly care about the welfare of others. It doesn't matter if you're a pastor, bishop, or chorister; if you don't love people, your religion is in vain!

Often, people say the word "I love you" without actually practicing it. Love is more than words; it is more about action (John 3:16).
Do you love people because of what they can offer, or do you love them because you're obeying God's commands?

Know that God sees your heart and knows your intentions.

Today, determined to spread the love of God to everyone you meet, whether they are believers or not. People are watching the way you interact with them. If you show genuine love and concern to them, they can decide to join the body of Christ.

Prayer Point: Father, thank you for sending your only Son to die for me on the cross of Calvary. In Jesus' Name, help me to love people the same way you love and care for me.

How can true believers know God loves them?

How do you show love to the people in your life? What is one thing you can start doing today to show love?

Day 6: Ask For God's Mercy

Bible Reading: Psalm 40:11

In our Bible reading today, the Psalmist asked God not to withhold His mercy from him. As believers, we need God's mercy to achieve everything good in life. Let's consider the story of Blind Bartimaeus as a case study (Mark 10:46-52).

Perhaps Bartimaeus was born blind or suddenly lost his sight; this detail isn't recorded in the Scriptures. But if you're familiar with this story, you'll understand that he was in distress.

Being blind turned Bartimaeus into a roadside beggar. Even if someone took all his earnings for the day, he wouldn't know. If he felt hungry, thirsty, or cold, he would have to ask people for help. Bartimaeus was completely dependent on people because he couldn't see.

One day, however, he heard that Jesus of Nazareth was nearby. In that moment, he shouted, "Jesus, Son of David, have mercy on me!" Many people told him to keep quiet, but he refused to remain silent because he was tired of his situation. That day, Bartimaeus's life changed because Jesus restored his sight.

Are you tired of the situation you are experiencing right now? Do you believe Jesus can change your life just as He changed Bartimaeus's life? If you have strong faith in God, ask Him for mercy. He will hear and respond to your prayers.

Prayer Point: Have mercy on me, Jesus, Son of David.

Describe a situation in your life where God has down mercy and compassion towards you.

What does mercy tell us about God's character?

Day 7: Who Are Your Friends?

Bible Reading: Proverbs 18:24

Friends play a significant role in our Christian journey. If the majority of your close friends are unbelievers, it is only a matter of time before you return to worldly ways.

Understand that there is nothing wrong with being friendly with unbelievers. However, you should set limits on your relationships with them. It is easier for them to influence you than for you to bring them to the kingdom, especially if you have all committed sins together in the past (1 Corinthians 15:33).

If you have recently given your life to Christ, attend a Bible-believing church and connect with like-minded people. The memory verse for today says, "One who has unreliable friends soon comes to ruin, but there is a friend who sticks closer than a brother." In other words, choose reliable friends if you want to avoid destruction in your life. Worldly friends can only bring pain, sorrow, and shame.

Read and reflect on God's word, pray, and spend time with other Christians to strengthen your relationship with Jesus Christ. He is the only one who sticks closer than a brother, father, mother, or sister.

Prayer Point: Heavenly Father, separate me from friends who will make me go back to my worldly ways. Connect me with people who will help me grow in my Christian journey in Jesus Name.

What have good friendships done for you in your life?

What kind of friendship do you have with Jesus? How has he been a good friend to you?

Day 8: Are You A Person Of Integrity?

Bible Reading: Proverbs 11:1

Nowadays, it is difficult to find people who are honest in their dealings. Therefore, believers should be among the few people who have integrity in the world today.

From our Bible reading for today (Proverbs 11:1), we can see that our God despises dishonest scales. But accurate weights find favor with him. In other words, God hates anything that involves cheating to maximize profits or to make progress. However, he will favor those whose dealings are right before him.

When God says he hates something, you should avoid it completely. If not, you will suffer serious consequences. In your place of work or neighborhood, can people testify that you're honest in your dealings? If your co-workers want to commit fraud, will they call you to join them?

Believe it or not, people watch your every move. They can easily identify those who are genuine children of God and pretenders. Let your speech and actions set you apart from the people of the world. Even if you are in a financial crisis, do not take actions that can tarnish your image.

Remember that a good name is more desirable than great riches, and being esteemed is better than silver or gold (Prov. 22:1).

Prayer Point: Father, help me to be a person of integrity so that I can receive favor from you in Jesus' Name.

Who do you know that is a person of integrity? What makes this person stand out from other people of similar age and position?

- --

Is it important for all black women to have high integrity? What is one moral principle you will NEVER break?

Day 9: You Can't Serve God And Money

Bible Reading: Matthew 6:24

Having enough money to cater to your needs, and those of your family creates a sense of safety. Even when financial needs continue to arise every day, you won't have to worry about how to meet them.

A part of God's plan for us as believers is to have everything we need to live a comfortable life. But when the love of money starts taking over your love for the things of God, there will be a problem.

There's no way you can serve God wholeheartedly when you're obsessed with chasing after money. If you're a true child of God, He will always ensure you have everything you need at the right time. But the problem most believers have these days is that they want to acquire more wealth.

Jesus told his disciples a parable about a rich man whose land produced an abundant harvest in Luke 12:16-21. In all this rich man's plans, he never included God or the less privileged. He was so confident in his money and planned to please himself for many years. But that night, God said the rich man's life would be demanded from him.

When God blesses you with wealth, He wants you to first acknowledge Him. He also wants you to remain humble so that you can continue to depend on Him. Furthermore, God wants you to use your money for the growth of His kingdom and to help the poor people around you. When you do all these, He will continue to ensure you don't lack anything good.

Prayer Point: Father, don't let the love of money take over the love I have for you in Jesus' Name.

How does your relationship to money relate to your identity?

Do you think the way you view money is the way God would want you to view it?

Day 10: Learn To Persevere

Bible Reading: Galatians 6:9

Perseverance is a key attribute that all believers should possess. Nothing good comes easily; you must put in time and effort no matter how difficult it appears.

There are several cases of people who persevered in the scriptures. Hannah was one of those mentioned in the Bible (1 Sam. 1:1). She desperately needed a child but couldn't conceive. To make matters worse, Hannah's rival, Peninnah, kept on mocking her. But this situation did not discourage her from praying to God. In the course of time, God heard and answered Hannah's prayers.

Another perfect example of someone who persevered in the scriptures is the Canaanite woman (Matt. 15:22–28). She knew Jesus could heal her demon-possessed daughter and wasn't ready to back down. Even when the responses she received were unfavorable, this woman continued to persuade Jesus to heal her daughter. Eventually, her request was granted because she didn't give up.

God doesn't want his children to fail in their endeavors. Therefore, when it looks as if there's a delay on your path to success, keep on pushing. With prayers, patience, and persistence, you will reach your desired goal.

Prayer Point: Father, give me the grace to persevere in my life endeavors. Help me to patiently wait for the breakthrough you have planned for me in Jesus' Name.

What does perseverance mean to you and how do you think it will help you throughout this life?

_____

_ _____

___ _____

_____

What is perseverance in prayer?

_____

_ _____

_____

Day 11: Flee From Sexual Immorality

Bible Reading: 1 Corinthians 6:18-20

When God gives a command, he wants us to obey it for our good. Sexual immorality comes with a lot of problems that can be avoided. Sexually pure believers do not engage in fornication, adultery, or pornography, homosexuality, and bestiality.

Sexual relations are beautiful in the sight of God only when two people who are legally married engage in them. If you're not careful, there are many ways in which you can fall into sexual temptation. But everything begins with the things you feed your mind.

The two major gateways by which information reaches our minds are through what we see and what we hear regularly. Do you enjoy watching certain types of movies or TV shows? Do you prefer to listen to worldly music rather than hear the word of God? Genuinely answer these questions and change your ways if you're guilty.

Perhaps you're struggling with sexual sins. Ask the Lord to set you free. Honor God with your body because you were bought at a price (1 Corinth. 6:20). Get rid of anything that causes you to constantly fall into sexual sin so that you can remain pure.

Prayer Point: Father, please help me to remain sexually pure in Jesus' Name.

How would you describe the culture's view of sex?

- --

--- --

Is sexual temptation an issue for you and if so how does this text help you to glorify God in your body?

- --

--- --

Day 12: How To Grow Spiritually

Bible Reading: 1 Corinthians 3:12-13

Just as we feed our physical bodies every day, we are supposed to nourish our spiritual bodies too. Babies need milk to grow, but as they grow older, they will need solid food to grow healthy.

When you do not feed on the word of God regularly, your growth will be stunted spiritually. It is no wonder that many believers are oppressed by the adversary all the time, despite looking healthy physically, they are weak spiritually.

From our Bible reading for today, Paul the Apostle described the believers of the Church of God in Corinth as mere infants of Christ. As a result, he gave them milk and no solid food because they could not handle it yet.

Spend quality time studying God's words to develop a good relationship with Him. While it can be tempting to eat every day of the week, you can set aside a day to fast. Instead of partying all night-long, spend some time praying for and interceding on behalf of others.

As you engage in these spiritual practices, you will begin to grow. When the devil wants to strike and sees you are fit spiritually, he will flee.

Prayer Point: Father, I don't want to be stagnant spiritually. Give me the grace to grow to full maturity in Jesus' Name.

Who are you sharing your beliefs with and what is the hardest challenge you are facing?

What are you praying about, and how is God working your life through prayer?

Day 13: Does God Care For Us?

Bible Reading: Matthew 6:25

Even when it doesn't look like it, God cares for us. Many of the verses in the Scriptures point to the fact that God genuinely loves his children. So if you're indeed a child of God, let this assurance be in your mind.

In the book of 1 Peter 5:7, the Lord Almighty asks you to cast your anxieties on Him because He cares for you. From our Bible reading for today, Jesus said we shouldn't worry about what to eat, drink, or wear. He has provided everything for us in abundance already.

One of the advantages of being a child of God is that He knows everything we need even before we ask. People in the world do not have this opportunity, and that's why their lives can be hard sometimes. All you need to do is seek God's kingdom and righteousness, and all these things will be given to you (Matthew 6:33).

Take a moment to think about the birds of the air, the fish of the sea, and the animals in the wild. They do not go to work or store food in the barns, but God feeds them every day. If God can do these things for animals, won't He do much more for the people who were created in His image and likeness?

Out of the love he has for humans, our God gave his only Son to die for our sins. Believe that there's no limit to the things He can give us.

Prayer Point: Father, thank you for loving and caring for me. Help me to completely depend on you for all my needs, in Jesus' name.

What are some ways you show appreciation to God?

What has happened in your life that has shown you that God cares about you?

Day 14: Living To Please God

Bible Reading: Romans 8:8

When you decide to please God, it means you are ready to obey all his commands. First, He will give you the grace to make this decision easily. Secondly, God will reward you for following His instructions.

There are lots of benefits to pleasing God with your life. He will make your enemies be at peace with you (Prov. 16:7). Also, you will always receive answers to your prayers (1 John 3:22). In addition, God will never leave you alone every day of your life (John 8:29).

Obeying God's commands requires determination. Many things in the world today will want to shift your attention away from the things of God. This is one of the plans of the devil to make you sin and offend God. Refuse to get carried away by the pleasures of the world, and your reward will come in no time.

Constantly read and meditate on the word of God daily so that you can be careful to do everything in it. Then you will be prosperous and successful (Josh. 1:8).

Prayer Point: Father, I desire to please you in all my ways. In the name of Jesus, help me to do what you say whether it's convenient or not.

Why is it easy to please people rather than God? Why is it so dangerous?

What does it mean to please God to you?

Day 15: How Does God Answer Our Prayers?

Bible Reading: 1 John 5:14

God loves to give His children what they ask for, and He will never keep anything good from a good person (Psalm 84:11). However, some factors can prevent you from receiving answers to your prayers.

Sin is one of the common reasons God may not hear your prayers (Psalm 66:18). Search your heart and turn a new leaf if you always commit a particular sin.

Also, when you pray, do you believe that God can answer your prayers? Some believers go to the Lord in prayer with doubts in their hearts. Then they begin to wonder why God has refused to grant their requests. People who have doubts in their minds should not expect to receive anything from God (James 1:7).

Another reason your prayers may be hindered is if your motives are wrong (James 4:3). God knows all things, and He can see all things. If He sees that you desire certain things for selfish reasons, He won't release them to you. Sometimes, you may not receive speedy answers to your prayers because God is teaching you how to be patient.

Contrary to the beliefs of certain people, prayer is not complicated. But you need to get it right before God can hear and answer you!

Prayer Point: Lord Jesus Christ, remove every
   hindrance to my prayers today. Grant all my heart's
desires and make my plans succeed.

How has God answered your prayers throughout your life?

How does God answer prayers in the Bible?

Day 16: When Do We Become Children of God?

Bible Reading: John 1:12

As a result of the fall of Adam in the Garden of Eden, everyone born into the world automatically inherits a sinful nature. No one has to teach little children how to behave wrongly; they know these things naturally. Unfortunately, unruly behaviors always lead to punishments such as jail terms, sickness, or death. But because God did not want us to perish, He sent His only Son to die for the sins of mankind.

All you need to do is to believe and receive Jesus Christ, the Son of God, as your Lord and Savior. Once you do this, you'll cross from darkness to light and become a child of God. While Adam's disobedience brought punishment into the world, Jesus Christ's obedience brought blessings to mankind. Hallelujah!

Now, to accept Jesus Christ as your Lord and Savior, you need to confess that He is Lord (Romans 10:9). You also need to believe in your heart that God raised Him from the dead and that you're now a child of God.

Romans 8:29 says that "For those God foreknew, He also predestined to be conformed to the image of His Son, that He might be the firstborn among many brothers and sisters." This means you're now related to Jesus Christ once you give your life to Him!

Prayer Point: Father, thank you for counting me worthy to be among your children. Continue to uphold me in my Christian race in Jesus' Name.

What does it mean to be a child of God?

What are some benefits of being a child of God?

Day 17: Why Do We Suffer?

Bible Reading: Romans 8:18

There's no doubt that our Heavenly Father loves and cares so much for His children. But sometimes, believers go through so much suffering and pain and keep on wondering why this happens.

God does not allow His children to go through difficult times without genuine reasons. Believers tend to move far away from God when they don't have anything to pray for.

Suffering and pain are two of the methods God employs to draw our attention back to Himself. This, however, does not imply that God willingly subjects His children to suffering. On the contrary, He wants us to depend totally on Him and to achieve certain purposes.

Suffering can come in the form of sickness, disease, lack of finances, relationship problems, and failures. One thing remains certain: this problem is only temporary; it will not last long (Psalm 30:5).

However, you need to make sure that the situation you're going through is not self-inflicted (Galatians 6:7). When you willingly cheat or hurt people, you will suffer the consequences.

Also, if you are sexually immoral and get a disease that is spread through sexual intercourse, it is all your fault.

Therefore, try to live a holy and obedient life. When you go through times of pain, go to the throne of mercy to ask for help, and God will answer you.

Prayer Point: Heavenly Father, give me relief from my pain. Help me to hold on to you through the good and bad times in Jesus' Name.

How has suffering throughout life make you as a person?

What do you believe is God's purpose in this suffering?

Day 18: How To Deal With Grief

Bible Reading: Psalm 86:7

When we suffer a significant loss, it is normal to grieve. While loss comes in different forms, some losses weigh us down more than others.

If believers applied for a huge contract and didn't get it, they may grieve for a while and move on. But if the same people lose a loved one, they will likely not get over it for a long time.

The loss of friendships, relationships, marriages, or jobs can also cause people to mourn. When Lazarus died, Our Lord Jesus Christ wept when he saw His loved ones weeping (John 11:35). This means that God knows the pain Believers go through when they suffer a loss. There is an assurance that He is always near to the brokenhearted and saves the crushed in spirit (Psalm 34:18).

In addition to healing the brokenhearted, God also binds up their wounds (Psalm 146:3).

If you're mourning the loss of something or someone dear to you, ask God to heal your wounds. You can also speak with a trusted friend or a counselor who will help you hasten the healing process.

Prayer Point: Father, I believe you're able to do all things. Today, heal my broken heart and fill my heart with peace and joy in Jesus' Name.

What spiritual lessons can we learn from life's losses and sorrows?

What are few ways the Bible shows how to deal with grief?

Day 19: How To Deal With Doubt

Bible Reading: James 1:16-8

Doubts are the opposite of faith. When you have doubts in your mind, it means you're telling God that he is unable to do what he says he'll do. That's disrespectful to the maker of heaven and earth!

Faith is the basis of Christianity. To have a relationship with God, you must believe in him completely. We can't see God face-to-face, but we believe he exists and can answer our prayers.

Sometimes, we exaggerate our situations and believe they are too big for God to handle. In the book of Mark 9:14–27, a caring father went to meet Jesus to heal his possessed son. The young boy had the evil spirit since he was a child and it frequently threw him into fire and water to kill him.

Due to the severity of the situation, the boy's father said to Jesus, "If you can do anything, take pity on us and help us." Jesus responded, "If you can? Everything is possible for one who believes." Eventually, the boy received his healing that day.

Whoever doubts can be compared to a wave of the sea blown and tossed by the wind (James 1:6). Unfortunately, they cannot receive anything from God.

If you're struggling with doubts, ask the Lord to help you overcome them. Always keep in mind that there's nothing God cannot do. Then go to him with all your needs, and he will meet them.

Prayer Point: Father, I believe there's nothing impossible for you to do. Please remove doubts from my heart so that my prayers will not be hindered in Jesus' Name.

What is the cause of doubt and how do you overcome it?

What are few ways the bible teaches us on how to deal with doubt?

Day 20: Are You Generous?

Bible Reading: Proverbs 11:24–25

Giving is one of the signs that you genuinely love people. God so loved the world that He gave His only Son (John 3:16). As a child of God, you need to follow in the footsteps of our Father in heaven.

Many people believe that if they give what little they have, it will finish quickly. But according to the Word of God, withholding what they have only leads to poverty (Proverbs 11:24).

When you give in the kingdom of God, it will be given to you. A good measure, pressed down, shaken together, and running over, will be poured into your lap (Luke 6:38).

There will always be poor people in your neighborhood, school, church, place of work, and every environment you find yourself in. When God blesses you, He wants you to bless these people as a way of showing genuine love.

Keep in mind that whoever is kind to the poor lends to the Lord, and He will reward them for what they have done (Proverbs 19:17).

Giving should not be a difficult task for you as a child of God. Don't wait until people beg and worship the ground you walk on before helping them. Make it a habit to give, beginning today, and God will reward you abundantly.

Prayer Point: Heavenly Father, thank you for blessing me in several ways. Give me the grace to be a blessing unto others in Jesus' Name.

Who in your life is someone that you would consider a generous person and how can you follow their footsteps?

How did Jesus demonstrate generosity?

Day 21: Strength In The Time Of Adversity

Bible Reading: Isaiah 40:29

At one time or another, you may feel physical, spiritual, and emotional weakness. When this happens, you need to go to God to draw strength.
There's a limit to what we can achieve on our own as humans. But sometimes, many believers try to handle life's challenges by themselves. Some of them even turn to the world to get relief and peace. Eventually, they will get overwhelmed by the troubling situation and feel worse than they did previously.

God is our refuge and strength, an ever-present help in trouble (Psalm 46:1). Whenever you feel down or weak in spirit, God's strength will replace your weakness if you call upon Him. There's nothing wrong with admitting that you are weak and need the help of the Almighty. No one in the world can give you peace like He will give you.

Stop burdening your mind with handling life's challenges alone; it will quickly drain you. Cast all your worries on the Lord, and He will sustain you. He will not let the righteous be shaken (Psalm 55:22).

Prayer Point: Father, strengthen me in times of weakness. Don't let me drown in life's challenges in Jesus' Name.

What are some ways to stay strong when time gets hard?

How do you overcome adversity according to the Bible?

Day 22: Learn To Be Patient

Bible Reading: Romans 8:25

Patience is a virtue, all true children of God should possess. When you exercise patience, it means you're humble enough to wait for what God has promised to accomplish.

Being patient means you are also mature enough to let go of certain unseemly behaviors instead of reacting (Prov. 16:32). People in the world may try to test your patience simply because you're a child of God. Don't allow them to make you sin against God.

Perhaps you're a single lady waiting to meet the love of your life, get married, and start a family. But none of the men you've been meeting are ready to get married, let alone start a family. And nearly all your close friends are meeting their prince charming and getting married every few months.

At this moment, you may begin to feel as though God has forgotten you. Understand that God makes everything beautiful in its time (Eccl. 3:11a). When you wait patiently for Him, He will never fail you.

While waiting for God to answer your prayers, have a positive attitude. Instead of complaining, be grateful to the Lord for the things He has done. Your attitude during the waiting period will determine how much time you spend in the situation. So, make a wise decision today!

Prayer Point: Heavenly Father, give me the spirit of patience today. Help me to hold on to your promises during my waiting period, in Jesus' Name.

In what area of your life are you struggling to deal with patience? Is there a particular person with whom you find it difficult to be patient?

What are the spiritual benefits of patience?

Day 23: Be Respectful

Bible Reading: 1 Peter 2:17

Everyone deserves to be respected, whether they are believers or not. Respect is a sign of humility. It means you don't see yourself as being better than others, regardless of your social status, wealth, beauty, intelligence, or achievement. Treat everyone as you want to be treated.

People who lack respect are considered rude. In the book of 1 Samuel 25, Nabal, who didn't reciprocate the humble approach of David's men but instead hurled insults at them and didn't offer them food and water, can be described as someone who lacks respect. Thanks to the respectful wife of Nabal, Abigail, who pleaded with David on his behalf. Eventually, the Lord struck Nabal, and he died, and David married Abigail.

There are many benefits that come from being a respectful individual, while disrespect has few.

As believers, always show people proper respect, even if you think they don't deserve it. This way, you will be able to preach the gospel to them freely, and they will listen to you.

Prayer Point: Father, help me to see everyone in your image and likeness. Give me the grace to honor and respect everyone in Jesus' Name.

Do you find it difficult to show respect in some situations? What can you do differently to show respect where it's due?

How did Jesus show respect to others throughout his life?

Day 24: Be Courageous!

Bible Reading: Deuteronomy 31:6

As with unbelievers, believers are constantly faced with life issues that can be overwhelming. God knows we will have trials and tribulations in different areas of life. It is for this reason that God commanded us, in His words, to always remain courageous. Even though it can be hard to have a positive mindset while going through difficult times, don't allow fear to take over your life.

When God sent Moses to Pharaoh to bring the children of Israel out of Egypt, his response was, "Who am I that I should go to Pharaoh and bring the Israelites out of Egypt?" This means Moses didn't believe he could be a savior to the Israelites.

Lack of courage is not from God; it is from the devil. Many people are struggling with fear and insecurities today because of the negative statements they've been exposed to at a young age. Some believers grew up in an environment where family members and friends kept reminding them of their failures. As a result of this, they have lost all sense of self-worth and are always timid among people.

Today, God is telling you to be courageous. From the time you became a follower of Christ, God has removed the spirit of timidity from you and replaced it with power, love, and self-discipline (2 Tim. 1:7).

Therefore, it is time to begin to act courageously everywhere you find yourself.

Prayer Point: Father, remove the spirit of timidity from my life and help me to be courageous from now, in Jesus' Name.

What is the one area of your life where you most need to display courage? Why?

What was Jesus facing that would take great courage, especially considering the fact that he knew exactly what would happen to him?

Day 25: Seek God's Wisdom

Bible Reading: James 1:5

To achieve anything meaningful in life, we all need the wisdom of God. It will help you to make the right decision, follow God's instructions, and live a long, prosperous, and healthy life.

King Solomon should have chosen wealth, fame, victory over his enemies, health, or other things, but he decided to choose wisdom. He knows that being a wise person opens the door to a wide range of benefits.

If you study the life of King Solomon in the book of 1 Kings 1–11, you will notice that he wasn't just wise, he was also one of the wealthiest men who ever lived. But that's not all! He was famous and had everything he needed in abundance, including wives and concubines.

If you desire the wisdom of God, have the fear of God in your heart (Prov. 9:10). Don't follow the way of the world. Then God will continue to save you from the troubles the people of the world are experiencing. If anyone lacks wisdom, they should ask God, who gives generously, and it will be given to them, according to James 1:5.

Since the Father has promised to make you wise if you desire it, why not go to Him in prayer today?

Prayer Point: Heavenly Father, give me the spirit of wisdom today in Jesus' name.

What is the best advice you have been given? How has this advice helped you?

In what ways have you seen biblical wisdom exemplified in another person?

Day 26: Don't Give In To Temptation

Bible Reading: 1 Corinthians 10:13

Despite being the Son of God, our Lord Jesus Christ was tempted by the devil in the wilderness (Luke 4:11–13). Hence, you will also face certain temptations at some point in your life. Most of the time, the devil tests believers with the things they need at a particular moment.

In the case of Jesus Christ, He needed food after fasting for 40 days and 40 nights. At that moment, the devil thought it was the right time to bargain with Him in exchange for bread. Unknown to the devil, Jesus Christ knew all the words of God it took to resist him.

As a believer, you need to invest your time and effort in studying the Word of God because temptations will come. And if you don't have knowledge of the Bible, the devil will perform his three-fold ministry on you: to steal, kill, and destroy (John 10:10).

Believers often fall into temptation when they're dragged away by their evil desires (James 1:14). Perhaps you're having financial trouble and your friends are suggesting illegal means to make money. Don't listen to them. Maybe you're married and one of your exes is asking you out on a single "harmless" date. Don't answer him. Whenever you want to sin, the devil will open your eyes to the "benefits" you would derive from it. Eventually, you would be full of regret if you decided to commit that sin. Remember, there's a way that appears to be right, but in the end, it leads to death (Prov. 14:12).

Prayer Point: Heavenly Father, I depend on your leadership and direction. No matter the situation I find myself in, don't allow me to fall into temptation in Jesus' Name.

Have you been tempted recently and how did you avoid it?

\---

\---

\---

What role does the word of God play in resisting temptation?

\---

\---

\---

Day 27: Major Keys To Marital Bliss

Bible Reading: Read Colossians 3:18

Marriage is a special institution that was designed by God. In Genesis 2:18, God said it is not good for man to be alone. None of the animals that God created were suitable for Adam. As a result of this, God created a woman for Adam to be his "helper." This is why a man leaves his father and mother and is united to his wife, and they become one flesh (Gen. 2:24).

Unfortunately, couples who are believers now go through a divorce when they have disagreements. Divorce is not God's plan for any of His children because it changes their lives forever. Permanent separation has effects on both the physical and psychological lives of the people involved, in addition to the social effects.

In Christian marriages, a wife should submit to her husband as it is fitting to the Lord. On the other hand, husbands should love their wives and shouldn't be harsh with them (Col. 2:18-19). In other words, the two major keys to marital bliss are love and submission.

Lots of marital problems, including divorce, can be avoided in Christian homes if couples can follow these divine instructions. Be your spouse's best friend. Even if there are conflicts between the two of you, resolve them as soon as possible. Practice loyalty, honesty, mutual respect, and understanding.

The devil loves it when couples have marital issues; don't allow him to destroy your home.

Prayer Point: Heavenly Father, let your peace and love continue to reign in my marriage. In Jesus' Name, don't allow the devil to gain an entrance into my family.

How can you avoid taking our loved ones for granted?

What is the meaning of headship and submission in the Bible and in our marriage?

Day 28: Find Out God's Will For Your Life

Bible Reading: Matthew 6:10

Knowing God's will for your life will prevent you from making costly mistakes. It is always better not to miss the path to a destination than to go back and retrace your steps. While some mistakes can be corrected, you may have to live with others for the rest of your life.

God's will regarding all life issues is in His word. So, if you want to know the mind of God about certain things, spend quality time studying His word. Sometimes, many believers make major decisions by themselves and then go to God for approval. When things don't go as planned, it is entirely their fault.

God doesn't reveal His will to just anyone. If you want to know his mind concerning any issue, you must have a cordial relationship with him. When you read your Bible daily, pray, fast, and fully obey God's instructions, He'll begin to reveal His plans for your life. He will also order your steps and direct your paths.

Are you planning to start a relationship that will lead to marriage? Find out the will of God. Do you want to change your career and don't know how to go about it? Find out God's plan.

In the book of Jeremiah 29:11, God says that the plans He has for you are to prosper you, not harm you. They are plans to give you hope and a future. Hold on to this word, and God will continue to unfold his plans for your life.

Prayer Point: Father, reveal the plans you have for every area of my life. Give me the grace to do your will even when it is not convenient for me, in Jesus' Name.

How do you know that what you desire is God's will?

What do you feel God's will is for you in this stage of your life?

Day 29: Teach Us How To Pray

Bible Reading: Matthew 6:9-13

Prayer is a mode of communication between God and man. As children of God, it is important to seek the face of God at all times through prayer. Constant communication with our maker draws us closer to him every day. If you have a friend who you talk to every day, it will be easier to approach him or her in your time of need. But if the only time you talk to one of your friends is when you have a need, they may not respond.

Communicating with your Heavenly Father should feel natural. God enjoys listening to and communicating with His children, through His words. Prayer is not an activity you engage in only when you have free time; it is a supernatural activity you should constantly engage in (1 Thes. 5:17).

But you need to learn the right approach to prayer so that you don't waste your time. When you want to pray, don't be like the hypocrites who love to be seen praying (Matt. 6:5). Go to a corner in your room and make your requests known to God. He will surely grant them.

Also, avoid repetition when praying. God knows what you need even before you ask. So don't think that babbling like unbelievers is all it takes to call God's attention.

Then follow the example of Jesus in prayer in the book of Matthew 6:9–13, and allow the Holy Spirit to minister to you.

Prayer Point: Heavenly Father, I depend on you to teach me how to pray. Help me to follow your divine instructions on prayers in Jesus' Name.

Do you pray to the lord once daily? What benefits do you get from daily prayer?

Do you feel more connected with Jesus Christ when praying?

Day 30: Just Obey

Bible Reading: Isaiah 1:19-20

Obedience is one way to show love and worship the Lord Almighty. It also enables you to confidently approach His presence to make known your requests. If you're a true child of God, obeying God should be a thing of joy because it is for your own benefit. He knows the paths that lead to life and the ones that lead to destruction. But one amazing thing about our God is that He doesn't force His children to obey Him; you must be willing.

Today, many believers only follow God's instructions when it is convenient for them. Some even obey partially, like King Saul in the book of 1 Samuel 15:7, who destroyed everything that was despised and considered weak, but spared the good ones. As a result of his disobedience, the Lord rejected him as the king of Israel.

God is more interested in your obedience than in offerings and sacrifices. As a result of disobedience, some believers have lost their wealth, ministry, health, opportunities, and other good things.

By reading and meditating on the Word of God, you will understand what you should and should not do. Decide to always obey God at all times, even when it is not easy.

Prayer Point: Heavenly Father, help me to
completely obey your commands so that I can lead a
healthy, peaceful, and long life in Jesus' Name.

*Has God ever directed you to do something you though
would be impossible? What was it?*

----

*Do you feel you can have more obedience
towards Christian values and lifestyle? How so?*

Made in the USA
Las Vegas, NV
21 July 2023